Monsieur Popotame

Gérard
Moncomble

Illustrations de
Pawel Pawlak

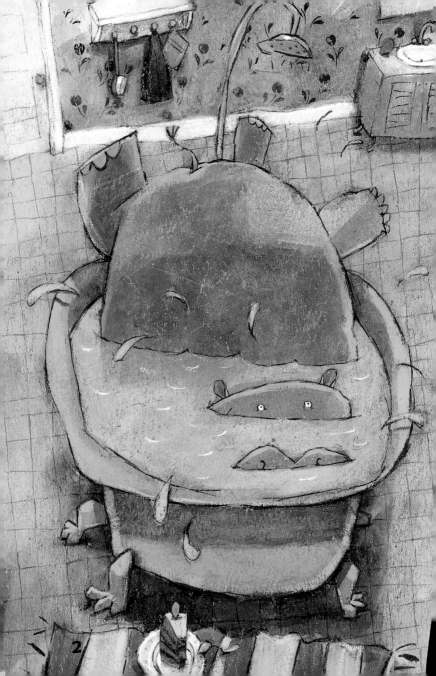

Chapitre 1

Monsieur Popotame passe
sa journée à manger et à dormir.
Entre deux miam-miam
et trois ron-ron-ron,
il **adooooore** prendre un bain.
Il barbote, il souffle
de l'eau avec
son nez, comme
les baleines.

Odile Croco, qui habite juste
en dessous, déteste qu'il pleuve
dans son thé. Elle cogne le plafond
avec son balai en hurlant :
– Assez de plouf-plouf-
plouf, là-haut,
    gros patapouf !

4

– Moi,
un gros patapouf ?
s'écrie monsieur Popotame.
Odile Croco est une langue
de vipère !

Mais dans l'escalier,
mam'zelle Gazelle dit d'un ton pincé :
– Vous prenez vraiment toute la place !
Heureusement que je suis mince
comme une guêpe !

Sur le trottoir,
tout le monde
s'écarte en ricanant.

— Gras de jambon !
chuchote Charly Chacal.

— Tonneau à pattes !
siffle Bill Boa.

— Bidon dodu !
murmure Zoé Zébu.

7

Monsieur Popotame s'inquiète.
Peut-être a-t-il quelques grammes
en trop. Il court chez le docteur Rhino,
qui est ca-té-go-ri-que :
– Trop gros, Popotame !
Beaucoup trop gros !

Monsieur Popotame doit faire
un régime pour maigrir.

Chapitre 2

Premièrement, il faut manger
un tout petit peu et même moins.
Deuxièmement, il faut faire beaucoup
d'exercice.
Troisièmement, il faut boire
énormément, énormément.
Ça marche ! Chaque jour, il maigrit
à vue d'œil !

Aujourd'hui, monsieur Popotame
se sent léger comme une libellule.
Il sort pour se faire admirer.
    Mais pourquoi mam'zelle Gazelle
        pousse-t-elle un cri d'horreur
            en le voyant ?

Pourquoi Odile Croco
ferme-t-elle ses volets ?

Pourquoi les passants
s'enfuient-ils ?

13

Voilà pourquoi.

Monsieur Popotame est devenu maigre à faire peur. Dans ses habits cent fois trop grands pour lui, sa peau pendouille comme un vieux drap usé.

– Quel horrible monstre !

murmure mam'zelle Gazelle.

« Moi, un horrible
monstre ? »
crie monsieur Popotame.
Lui qui croyait faire plaisir
à tout le monde !

Et il court
se cacher au fond
de son appartement.

15

Chapitre 3

À présent, dans le quartier,
personne n'ose mettre le nez dehors.
Odile Croco dit qu'il vole au-dessus
de la ville, avec ses ailes de dragon !
Mam'zelle Gazelle raconte
qu'il crache des flammes
quand il est en colère.

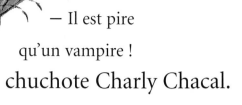

— Il est pire
qu'un vampire !
chuchote Charly Chacal.

— Plus affreux
que Barbe-Bleue !
siffle Bill Boa.

— Un diable !
Épouvantable !
Abominable !
glapit Zoé Zébu.

Comment s'en débarrasser ?
Tout le monde se met à réfléchir.

Odile Croco a une idée :
– On pourrait l'amadouer.
Qu'est-ce que ça aime, les monstres ?
– Monsieur Popotame adooooore
les gâteaux ! dit mam'zelle Gazelle.
Et ils galopent tous à la pâtisserie.

19

Driiinngg !

Dans son réfrigérateur,
monsieur Popotame
dresse l'oreille.
Qui sonne à la porte ?
Une voix crie :
– On a une
surprise
pour vous,
cher voisin !

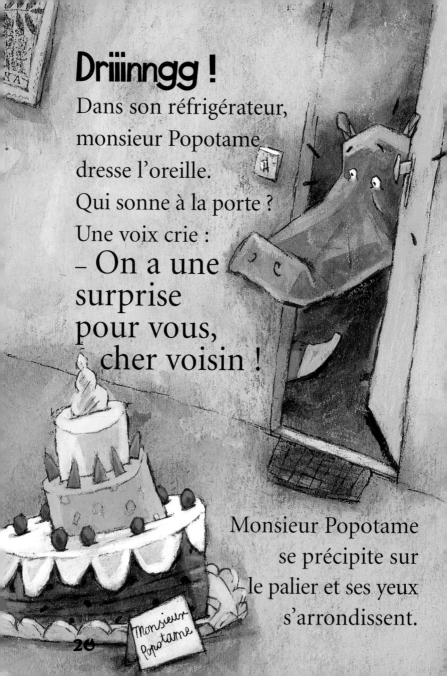

Monsieur Popotame
se précipite sur
le palier et ses yeux
s'arrondissent.

Monsieur
Popotame

20

Monsieur Popotame reprend
des forces. Monsieur Popotame
reprend des formes.
Monsieur Popotame
reprend goût
à la vie.

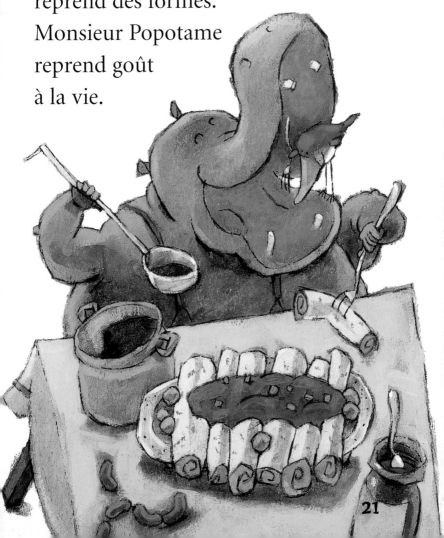

Le monstre a disparu. Tout le quartier respire. Et quand il pleut chez Odile Croco, elle sourit en disant :
– Tiens, je crois que notre cher monsieur Popotame prend son bain !

FIN

23

© 2000 Éditions MILAN
300, rue Léon-Joulin, 31101 Toulouse cedex 9 – France
Droits de traduction et de reproduction réservés pour tous les pays.
Toute reproduction, même partielle, de cet ouvrage est interdite.
Une copie ou reproduction par quelque procédé que ce soit,
photographie, microfilm, bande magnétique, disque ou autre,
constitue une contrefaçon passible des peines prévues
par la loi du 11 mars 1957 sur la protection des droits d'auteur.
Loi 49.956 du 16.07.1949
Dépôt légal : 1er trimestre 2006
ISBN : 2-7459-0056-0
www.editionsmilan.com
Imprimé en France par Fournié

SPACE STATIONS

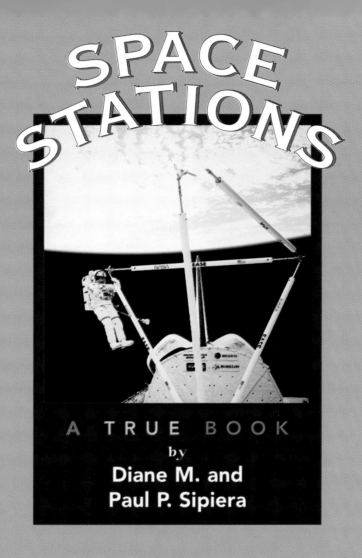

A TRUE BOOK

by

**Diane M. and
Paul P. Sipiera**

Children's Press®
A Division of Grolier Publishing

New York London Hong Kong Sydney
Danbury, Connecticut

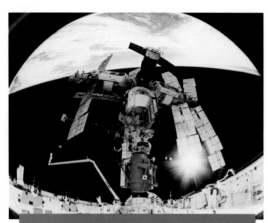

Space station *Mir* and
space shuttle *Atlantis*

Subject Consultant
Peter Goodwin
Science Department Chairman
Kent School, Kent, CT

Reading Consultant
Linda Cornwell
Learning Resource Consultant
Indiana Department
of Education

Authors' Dedication:
To Byron K. Lichtenberg—
astronaut, visionary,
and friend

Library of Congress Cataloging-in-Publication Data

Sipiera, Diane M.
    Space stations / Diane M. Sipiera and Paul P. Sipiera.
    p. cm.— (A true book)
    Includes bibliographical references and index.
    Summary: Examines space stations past and future and discusses their
contributions to the exploration of worlds beyond our own.
    ISBN 0-516-20450-5 (lib. bdg.)   0-516-26277-7 (pbk.)
    1. Space stations—Juvenile literature. [1. Space stations. 2. Outer
space—Exploration] I. Sipiera, Paul P. II. Title. III. Series.
TL797.S55   1997
629.44'2—dc21
                                                        97-3662
                                                          CIP
                                                          AC

Contents

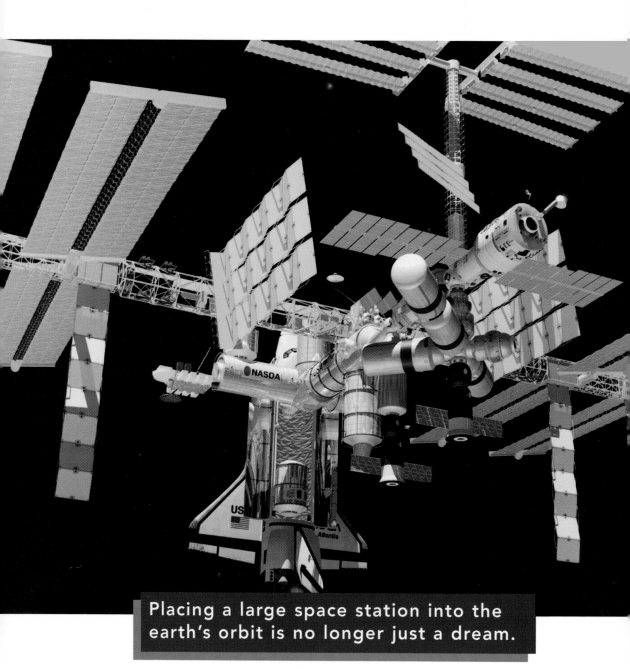

Placing a large space station into the earth's orbit is no longer just a dream.

Exploring Space

For many years, people have dreamed about exploring space. Some science fiction writers imagined huge space stations orbiting the earth, where people would live and work. They imagined that travel to the station would be like an airplane flight from Chicago to New York. Today, this dream is coming true.

Why do we want to go into space? Throughout history, people always have had the desire to see new places. Some people wanted to find better lands in which to live. Some were forced to leave their homes by enemies. Some just wanted to explore.

Today, almost every place on Earth has been explored, so we look to space. People have landed on the Moon and explored other planets

Someday, people may be living on the Moon (above) or Mars (right).

with spacecraft. Perhaps someday soon, people will be living on the Moon or on Mars. The first step to further space exploration is to build a space station in the earth's orbit. There, people will learn how to live in space.

Living in Space

In 1961, Yuri Gagarin was the first person to orbit the earth. He spent about ninety minutes in space. Those who followed stayed for longer periods of time. Scientists have found that the human body changes the longer it stays in space. After returning from long flights, some astronauts have

People and objects
appear to float in space.

trouble standing up and walk-
ing. So far, the longest time
anyone has spent in space is
just over one year. But when
that cosmonaut returned to
Earth, he needed over six
months to regain his strength.

Living in space is very dif-ferent from living on Earth. Gravity (or the pull of the earth on our bodies) makes our bones and muscles strong. But in space, the force of gravity is very weak. The heart does not work as hard. Muscles become weak because movement requires little effort. Bones also become weak because the body loses calcium. Therefore, as space stations become a

An astronaut works outside the spacecraft (above). These astronauts (right) try to eat their meals in a weightless environment.

reality, scientists are carefully watching how the human body acts in space. They are developing new training methods for the astronauts as well.

11

The First Space Stations

The first space station was called *Salyut 1*. It was launched in April 1971 by the Soviet Union. Three cosmonauts in the *Soyuz 11* spacecraft docked with the *Salyut 1* space station and lived in it for twenty-four days. Tragically, all three men died

A *Salyut*
space station

when they tried to return to
Earth. There were six more
Salyut space stations, and all
were very successful.
Cosmonauts on board the

13

stations performed many scientific experiments, such as testing the effects of weightlessness on the human body.

The first U.S. space station program was Project Skylab. The National Aeronautics and Space Administration (NASA) used extra rockets from the Project Apollo moon missions (1967–72) to make *Skylab* and launch it into space in 1973.

The *Skylab* space station was manned by three crews of

The *Skylab* space station weighed 100 tons (91 metric tons). The astronauts lived and worked in an area 48 feet (15 meters) long and 22 feet (7 m) wide.

three astronauts each. The first crew was in orbit around the earth for just over twenty-eight days. Its main mission was to repair the damage that occurred shortly after

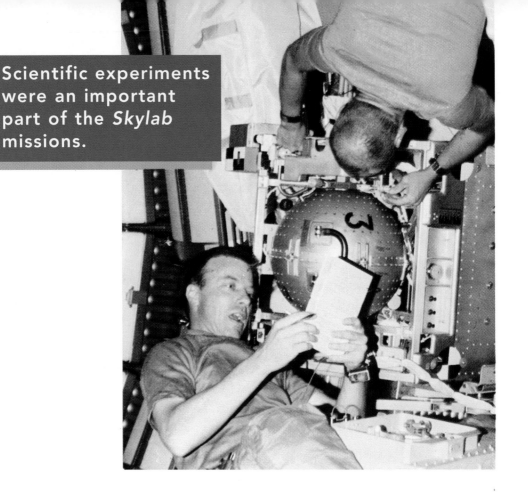

Skylab's launch. A rocket blast had torn off one of the station's two big solar panels and its heat shield. The second mission lasted over fifty-nine days. During that time, the astronauts conducted many medical and scientific experiments. The final mission took eighty-four days.

The *Skylab II* crew included (from left to right) Owen K. Garriott, Jack R. Lousma, and Alan L. Bean.

The *Skylab III* astronauts saw Comet Kohoutek.

The highlight of the last mission was observing Comet Kohoutek. Together, the three *Skylab* missions provided NASA with a lot of scientific information. *Skylab* disintegrated when it reentered the earth's atmosphere in 1979.

Space Shuttles

NASA needed to find better ways to travel into space. The huge rockets that took astronauts to the Moon during Project Apollo were very expensive and could be used only once. President Richard M. Nixon directed NASA to build space shuttles. These

Space shuttles are reusable. Powerful rockets launch them into space (right), and parachutes help slow their landing (below).

spacecraft would be able to travel into space and then return to Earth, perhaps as often as twice a month. NASA hoped that the space shuttles could one day be used to build a permanent space station.

There were many delays in the space shuttle program right from the start. The first shuttle flight took place on April 12, 1981. It lasted just over fifty-four hours. Twenty-three missions followed before

The crew of the space shuttle *Challenger*

an accident with the space shuttle *Challenger* took the lives of seven astronauts. Since then, many improvements have been made to the shuttle, and the space shuttle astronauts have carried out many important missions.

Today, space shuttle astronauts are practicing to build
an international space station.
Once construction of the
space station begins, the

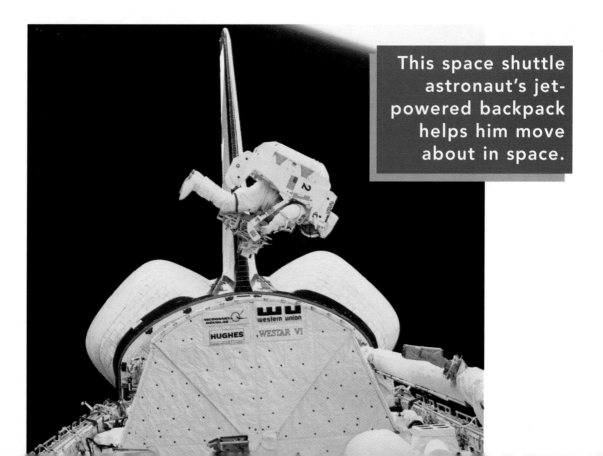

This space shuttle
astronaut's jet-
powered backpack
helps him move
about in space.

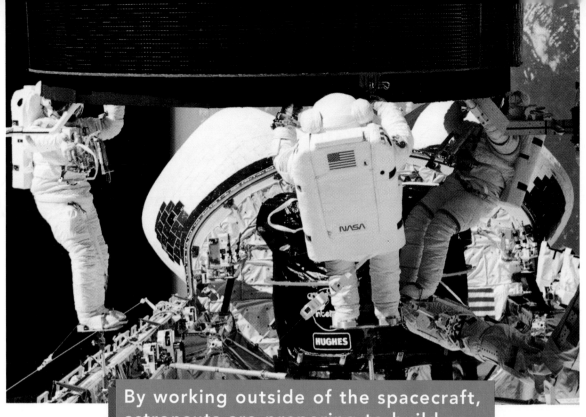

By working outside of the spacecraft, astronauts are preparing to build an international space station.

astronauts will spend a great
deal of time outside the shuttle
putting parts of the station
together. They will need to
learn how to work in space.

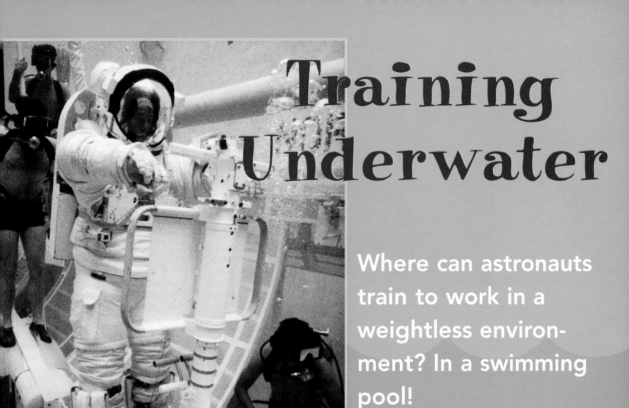

Training Underwater

Where can astronauts train to work in a weightless environment? In a swimming pool!

By practicing their tasks underwater, the astronauts are well prepared to work while floating in space.

Space Station *Mir*

Today, the Russian space station *Mir* (meaning "peace") is orbiting the earth. It was launched in February 1986. On board, there is generally a crew of two cosmonauts with an occasional visiting astronaut from the United States.

Mir was designed so that
up to six extra sections could
be added to its basic design.
Recently, U.S. space shuttles

On board space
station *Mir*

have been joining up with *Mir*
to exchange crews. Together,
the American astronauts and
Russian cosmonauts are practicing for construction of the
International Space Station—
a project planned since 1984.

Success will depend on how well they work together.

People on Earth can see *Mir* at night as it passes overhead. It looks like a bright star moving quickly from west to east.

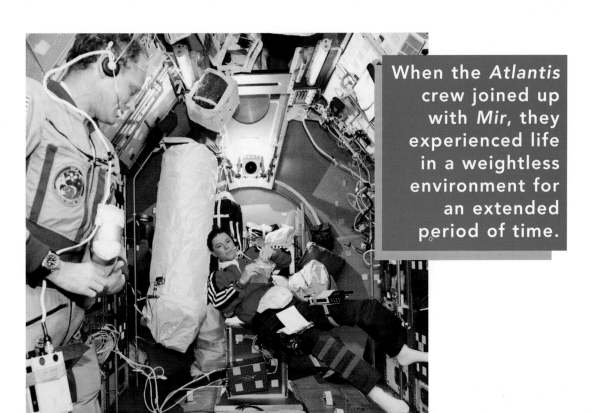

When the *Atlantis* crew joined up with *Mir*, they experienced life in a weightless environment for an extended period of time.

Working Together

Mir has been a very important step in bringing the space programs of Russia and the United States together. One visitor to the Russian space station, Shannon Lucid (below), stayed for six months and served with four mission commanders. Her stay was the longest an American astronaut has ever spent in space.

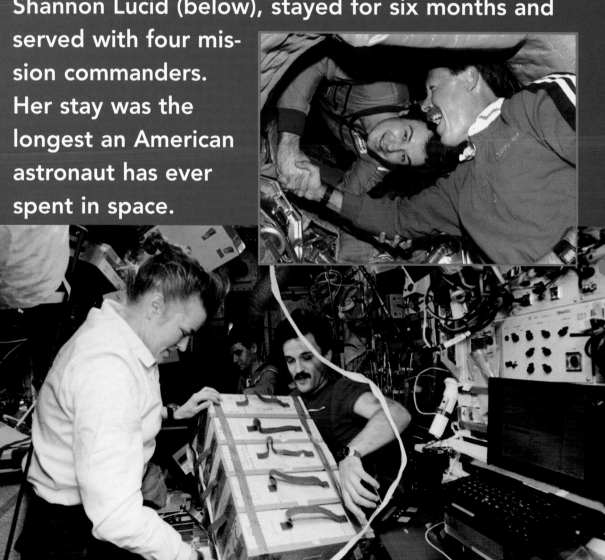

The International Space Station

On January 25, 1984, President Ronald Reagan announced a plan to build a permanent space station called Space Station *Freedom*. It was designed for a crew of eight people.

Since the station's first designs were drawn, many

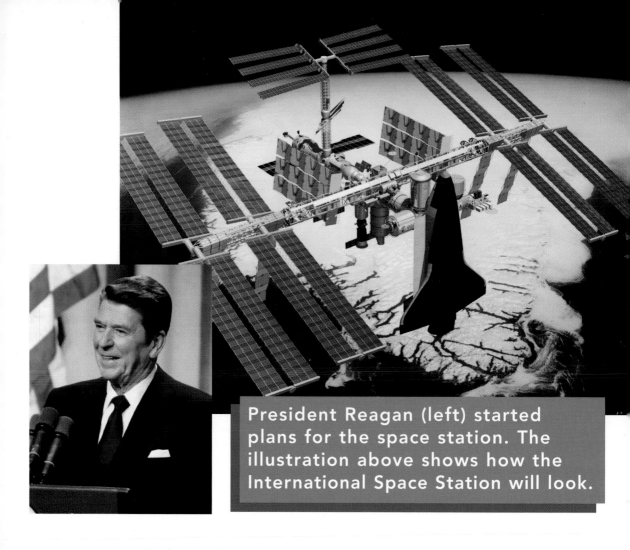

President Reagan (left) started plans for the space station. The illustration above shows how the International Space Station will look.

things have changed. The plans were completely redone in 1993. To help keep the cost low, certain parts were left out or redesigned. Other countries also were invited to join the United States. Thirteen nations now participate in the program. As a result, the station has been renamed the International Space Station.

If there are no more delays, assembly of the International Space Station will soon begin and will take about five years to complete. There will be thirty-six U.S. and Russian launches to assemble the station. Additional launches will be needed to re-supply it with food, water, fuel, and scientific equipment once it is in operation.

The first part of the station to be launched will be made by the Russians. Part of it will be a living space for the astronauts. It will also be the control and command center. A part made by the United States will soon follow. It is hoped that after

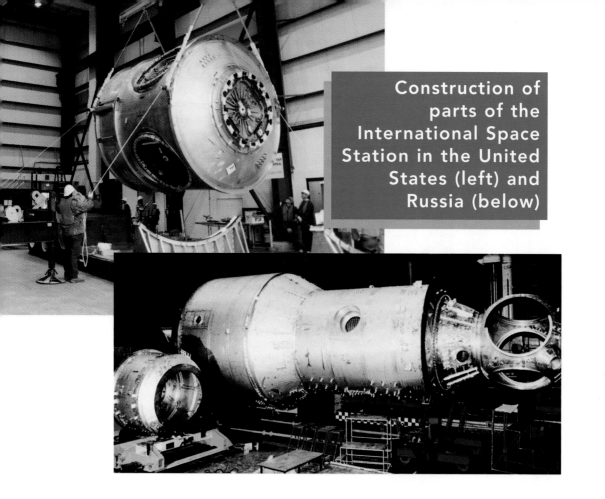

only four assembly missions, a working space station for up to three people will be in operation. Once completed, the station will support a crew

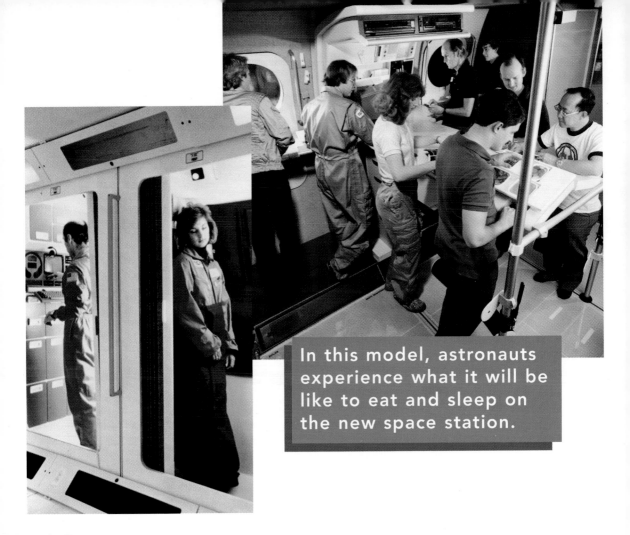

In this model, astronauts experience what it will be like to eat and sleep on the new space station.

of six, with room for up to fifteen when the space shuttle is visiting. The crew will change every three months.

International Space Station FACTS

The lifetime of the station will be ten years.

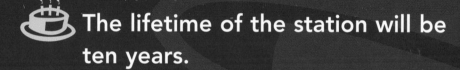

The station will travel around the earth at about 18,000 miles (29,000 kilometers) per hour. It will complete one orbit every 90 minutes.

Astronauts will "visit" with their family and friends on two-way television sets.

The crew will use a shower that looks like a car wash for people. They will be sprayed with water while fans blow the water toward the drains.

More than 95 percent of the world's population will be able to see the station in the sky. It will look like the brightest star just before sunrise or just after sunset moving from west to east.

Uses for the Space Station

Once the International Space Station is in operation, it will have many uses. In the area of space exploration, the station will be used as a place to assemble spacecraft headed to the Moon or Mars. Instead of launching one large spacecraft from Earth, it would cost

The experience that shuttle astronauts have had working in space will prepare them to assemble spacecraft at the space station.

much less money to launch several small sections of it. Then, at the space station, these parts could be put together to make the larger spacecraft.

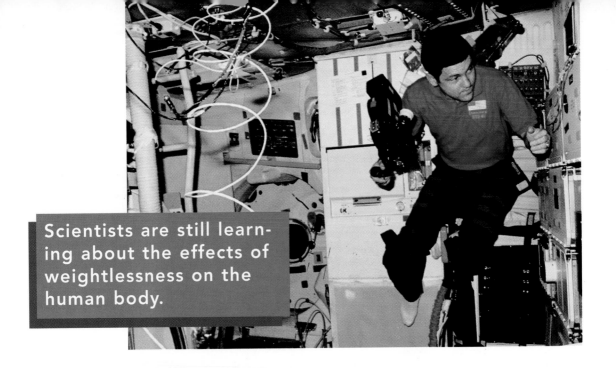

Scientists are still learning about the effects of weightlessness on the human body.

The space station will also be used to train astronauts for long space flights. Scientists will study how to overcome the effects of weightlessness on the human body. The lessons learned will also help the space explorers live normal lives after they return to Earth.

Weather patterns and entire continents can be seen clearly from space.

Other people will also have
uses for the International Space
Station. From orbit, scientists
will study weather patterns and
ocean currents. They will be
able to protect the environment
by finding sources of pollution.

Geologists will see entire continents at one time. This will help them understand how the earth changes. Astronomers will have the best view of space. There is no telling what discoveries they might make.

Space stations may also be used by industry. There are many things that can be made better in space than on Earth, such as medicine and the crystals used in electronics. Some people hope that a space station will collect sunlight and beam it back to Earth, where it could be turned into electricity. There are many different ways the space station will benefit people on Earth.

Space stations will give people the chance to explore new worlds and discover what lies beyond the planet Earth.

To Find Out More

Here are more places to learn about space exploration:

 **Books**

 **Organizations**

Kerrod, Robin. **The Story of Space Exploration.** Dutton Children's Books, 1994.

Kettelkamp, Larry. **Living in Space.** Morrow Junior Books, 1993.

Richardson, James. **Science Dictionary of Space.** Troll Associates, 1992.

Sipiera, Diane M., and Paul P. **The Hubble Space Telescope.** Children's Press, 1997.

Sipiera, Diane M., and Paul P. **Project Apollo.** Children's Press, 1997.

NASA Teacher Resource Center
Mail Stop 8-1
NASA Lewis Research Center
21000 Brookpark Road
Cleveland, OH 44135
(216) 433-4000

National Space Society
922 Pennsylvania Ave. SE
Washington, DC 20003
(202) 543-1900

National Air and Space Museum
Smithsonian Institution
601 Independence Ave. SW
Washington, DC 20560
(202) 357-1300

Online Sites

The Children's Museum of Indianapolis
http://childrensmuseum. org/sq1.htm

Visit the SpaceQuest Planetarium to see what it has to offer, including a view of this month's night sky. It can connect you to other astronomy Web sites, too.

History of Space Exploration
http://bang.lanl.gov/ solarsys/history.htm

This site has a helpful timeline of space exploration and tells the history of the spacecraft and astronauts.

Kid's Space
http://liftoff.msfc.nasa.gov/ kids/welcome.html

Space exploration is really fun at this Web site. Find out how much you would weigh on the Moon, play games, solve puzzles, take quizzes, read stories, and look at the gallery of pictures drawn by kids. Find out how you can post a drawing online, too!

NASA Home Page
http://www.nasa.gov

Visit NASA to access information about its exciting history and present resources.

Important Words

astronomer a scientist who studies the
   stars and planets

atmosphere layers of gases that surround a
   planet

comet an object with a long tail that orbits
   around the sun

cosmonaut a Russian space traveler

dock to join together

geologist a scientist who studies rocks,
   minerals, and landforms

mission a goal for spacecraft or astronauts
   to accomplish

orbit the path a spacecraft travels around
   the earth

rocket a powerful vehicle that launches
   spacecraft into space

weightlessness the appearance of astronauts and objects floating in space

Index

Meet the Authors

Paul and Diane Sipiera are a husband and wife who share interests in nature and science. Paul is a professor of geology and astronomy at William Rainey Harper College in Palatine, Illinois. He is a member of the Explorers Club, the New Zealand Antarctic Society, and was a member of the United States Antarctic Research Program. Diane is the director of education for the Planetary Studies Foundation of Algonquin, Illinois. She also manages and operates the STARLAB planetarium program for her local school district.

When they are not studying or teaching science, Diane and Paul can be found enjoying their farm in Galena, Illinois, with their daughters, Andrea, Paula Frances, and Carrie Ann.